DON'T FORGET ME

Slowly Slipping Away

Dean Parrish
Donetta Bennett Harned
de de Cox

DON'T FORGET ME

Quantity sales and special discounts are available on quantity purchases by corporations, associations, and others. For details, contact the publisher at the address above.

Orders by U.S. trade bookstores and wholesalers. Email info@ BeyondPublishing.net

The Beyond Publishing Speakers Bureau can bring authors to your live event. For more information or to book an event contact the Beyond Publishing Speakers Bureau speak@BeyondPublishing.net

The Author can be reached directly at BeyondPublishing.net

Manufactured and printed in the United States of America distributed globally by BeyondPublishing.net

BEYOND
PUBLISHING

New York | Los Angeles | London | Sydney

ISBN: 978-1-637923-63-4

TABLE OF CONTENTS

SISTERS, SISTERS,… DEVOTED SISTERS

I want to dedicate this book to my sister, Casonya Coomes Ritchie.

This is my entire life with her. We were never apart. If we were, we would find each other or sense that the other needed them. Since I am the oldest, she has been with me all my life. Growing up on the farm, there are pictures of chest drawers with both she and I sleeping together in this piece of furniture. You see, our claim to fame is we are one year, one month, one day, one hour, one minute apart from each other in our birthdays. She has black hair. I have blonde. Growing up, our momma always made our clothes. We were made to look like twins. It was incredible how much we did look like each other when we were younger. As we grew and began elementary school, Momma was there to create and sew, not just for us, but for others, too. The picture is our school Christmas play. We were angels. Momma made these dresses. My sister and I, as close as we are, are very different. We've each chosen different paths with family and with life, but we've never left each other. We actually work together. These past three years have been the hardest. You could describe some days as "pure hell". I don't know that I could be the person I am today if it were not for her. We've argued and disagreed so much over our momma and this disease, dementia. At times it has literally separated us and placed a wedge in between our relationship as sisters but GOD always brings us back together. There have been moments we have screamed and cried. There have been moments we have laughed at the disease and what it has done to take our momma away. AND then there are the moments where we look at each other and a tear trickles down, and we just know. This disease doesn't stop. And neither have we. She is my sister. She is the one who understands me better than anyone else. She is my sister. I love her.

I want to dedicate this book to my mom, Dorothy Parrish. Mom was married to Dad for a little over fifty-nine years at the time of his death. The mere fact that they stayed together all those years is a real testament to the level of commitment and fortitude that it takes to make a marriage last that long. I know from being there and experiencing it firsthand that it wasn't easy. There were many challenges and struggles along the way. The greatest of these struggles came in the form of Dad's diagnosis, first with an unspecified form of Dementia, then later, Alzheimer's. I watched Mom stay by his side as Dad continued to slip away. I saw her cry tears of anger, hurt and frustration as the man she loved and married was slowly taken from her. She lost the man many times over before he finally passed after battling this dreadful disease for over five years. As Dad's primary caregiver, Mom seemed to become a prisoner in her own home as he would eventually require around-the-clock care. Mom couldn't leave the house unless someone was there to care for him. Near the end, she never left the house and seldom got any breaks. As a family, we pitched in as much as possible. Ultimately, the mental and physical exhaustion took a heavy toll on her. She found inspiration from scripture and kept this verse on her refrigerator:

"It is of the LORD's mercies that we are not consumed, Because his compassions fail not. They are new every morning: Great is thy faithfulness. The LORD is my portion, saith my soul; Therefore will I hope in him."

"It is of the LORD's mercies that we are not consumed, Because his compassions fail not. They are new every morning: Great is thy faithfulness. The LORD is my portion, saith my soul; Therefore will I hope in him." Lamentations 3:22-24 KJV

What a tremendous example of selfless love. You are a true inspiration for me and countless others. Thank you, Mom. Love you.

I would like to dedicate this book to one of the most selfless, supportive, caring humans, I have ever known. I proudly get to call her my momma. Mary Etta Proffitt Bennett, has always been strong in her Godly beliefs. She taught us as young children, about God's word and worshiping in the house of God every Sunday. She has worked very hard to keep our family close.

She always shared her knowledge and wisdom, which has helped us each grow into responsible and respectful adults.

She and our father, Donnie, have been married for 62 years. There have been many ups and downs throughout their marriage, but she has honored her vows," in sickness and in health, til death do us part".

She has always been the main supporter in our family. As a child, I cannot remember her ever missing any event or program, while staying involved every step of the way. She taught us that we should always complete what we started. She has done the same with her grandchildren and now her great-grandchildren. Family is most important to her. This sassy little lady, at nearly eighty years young, can literally work circles around me and most adults. She is determined to try to do everything for herself, whether she needs to or not. She is very independent, a wee bit stubborn and has a little trouble admitting she is ever wrong, and most of the time, she is correct. With our mom, all you ever had to do is call, and she would drop whatever she was doing to come help or just support us kids. She has continued her caring and support with her grandchildren as well.

Lord knows that she is going over and above in the care giving to our daddy right now. We never in a million years, thought we would all have to take the responsibility of caring for our daddy. Our mother has been amazing in the nurturing and now the protector of her husband. She is not always the most patient, with the mind health of her husband now, which I understand completely.

She has always been very active outside the home. She worked very hard in her gorgeous and tidy vegetable gardens. Always raking, tilling, hand hoeing out the weeds, even down to picking and everything in between. She often ended up giving most of it away to her kids. In the hot summer, she would be out very early in her garden, before the heat set in, and would accomplish more by 10:00 in the morning than I would all day.

At one time, she was an avid golfer, playing for fun and exercise, and social time away. She joined golf leagues in her mid 30's until finally hanging her clubs up at the age of 76. She also has enjoyed being on a bowling league for several years. She enjoyed going on her bowling trips, mainly to Nevada. She had to put her bowling fun on hold, at the age of 80, due to hip replacement, but has every intention of going back. She has always been a people person with a gift for gab. She could go up to just about anyone and strike up a conversation.

She would know that person's life story by the time they finished their conversation. She just has a way of communicating with people and seems to truly care about others' lives and stories. We (her kids) always said she should have had a career as a detective. She has a way of dragging information out of you before you could blink your eyes without you realizing it. If she was ever unsure of anything, she would read, research, ask a million questions until she had her questions answered, which is a credit to her intelligence on many subjects. She wouldn't give up on anything until she was satisfied. Her ability to remember things always amazes me. She recalls times, places, and every single little detail. I'm truly jealous of this special gift that she still has, to be able to remember so much.

She and I have had many ups and downs because we are alike in many ways. As I have grown older and wiser, I know for sure that this lady has been an amazing rock in our family. We are truly blessed to have this strong, reliable lady to raise us. I pray that I can be half the lady, mother, and wife she has been. Thank you, a million times over.

I love you always, my wonderful momma.

CHAPTER ONE

RENEWAL

My Dad was a strong and hardworking man. Some would call him a gentle giant. He was so tall he had to duck to get through doors. His hands were huge and weathered from hard work. Dad ventured into his own business by purchasing a bulldozer and worked long tiresome hours to support his family. His business grew and he eventually purchased another dozer, grader, backhoe, and dump truck. He taught me to operate equipment of all kinds as well as how to work on it. Dad was not what you would call a well-educated man as he only completed 6th grade. However, his knowledge surpassed many who acquired a college education. His wisdom of the outdoors and excavation were gained by experience and hands on self-learning. He taught me more than I could ever learn from a textbook and that is the reason I'm a crane operator today. Throughout his years as a business owner, he always operated with honesty and integrity. Perhaps that's the reason he never got rich but always managed to provide.

Dad loved his grandchildren with his whole heart. He often picked my girls up when they got off the bus and took them to the food mart to buy them whatever snacks they wanted. He always emptied his pockets of change for them to add to their piggy banks. He was a very generous man and always slipped me money when Mom wasn't around. He would give to anyone in need. Dad envisioned his family enjoying the land he had worked for and therefore, built a lake for recreation and now his children, grandchildren and great grandchildren are reaping the rewards.

I can't say my dad was always perfect. He had a drinking problem for years and never attended church with mom and me.

He enjoyed music and cutting a rug at a good party. In 1998 he had a dream and saw a woman standing at the foot of his bed. He never elaborated on the details but the next morning he went to church and never drank again. I have to believe God sent an angel that night and Dad spent the rest of his life serving our Lord and Savior. He was an essential role in establishing Boston

Community Church. He witnessed to others every chance he got. HIs life was a true testimony of what God can do.

As Dad began to fade away to Alzheimer's he was often confused and forgetful, but the one thing he was never confused about was his love for Christ. Even in his weakest state he witnessed to the staff in the hospital and nursing facility.

A hard-working man with an amazing life, a true testimony, a love for Christ, family and others, and a gentle giant. That was my dad and that's how I will always remember him.

Submitted by Tim & Jennifer V.

"A good man leaves an inheritance to his children's children, And the wealth of the sinner is stored up for the righteous." Proverbs 13:22 NASB1995

"He who is generous will be blessed, For he gives some of his food to the poor." Proverbs 22:9 NASB1995

"Whatever you do, do your work heartily, as for the Lord rather than for men, knowing that from the Lord you will receive the reward of the inheritance. It is the Lord Christ whom you serve." Colossians 3:23-24 NASB1995

NOTES:

_____

_____

_____

_____

_____

_____

_____

_____

_____

_____

_____

_____

_____

_____

_____

_____

_____

_____

_____

_____

Dementia gave me my mom back. My mother came from an abusive background. So, naturally, that filtered into my childhood. My mother was not nice, yelled (a lot), was never warm, never positive, never hugged me, and rarely played. It took me many, years to understand this cycle and once I grew into adulthood, eventually set firm boundaries. For a time before her illness, I did not see her in person and rarely spoke to her on the phone.

Eventually due to years of poor self-care, she developed diabetes and dementia. My aunt found her in a diabetic induced coma on the floor of her kitchen. Due to her mental state, she could no longer live on her own and administer insulin. My mother was placed in a long-term care facility where she remained until her death in May of 2020.

In February of 2020 I began to regularly visit the nursing home due to my mom's declining health. She could not understand why she could not go back to her home, often asked if I was watering her plants, and never did comprehend why we placed her with all those 'old' people. The first week of March my mother was sitting on the edge of the bed. I was getting ready to leave but her next words caused a sharp jolt that penetrated to my core. This harsh, negative woman looked at me with clarity and said words I had never heard from her before – I'm sorry. As I sat there next to her on the bed, words came tumbling forth from her mouth. Apology after apology for the ways I had been treated. Sincere expressions of regret for things done in moments past. Tears for time that has been missed. I remember looking at her and honestly asking why she had not said these things sooner; why she had waited so long to say so many needed things. From then on, we talked daily and visited frequently. For the last few months of her life, I had the mom I had always wanted and needed, but never had.

March 9th was her birthday. That was also the last day I was able to see her in person before the nursing home was put on lock down due to Covid. From March the ninth until her death on the first day of May, we talked daily on the phone. A dementia patient in lock down is an interesting conversation. Some days she was very clear-headed and reiterated that the facility had plenty of toilet paper. (She asked the head nurse one day – just to be sure.) Other days I had to yell into the mouthpiece to have her turn the phone around. Holding it upside down and still trying to carry on a conversation was one of her dementia induced specialties those final weeks. Many days (both in and outside of the dementia haze) she exhibited frustration that we could not come in to see her. The feeling was mutual. On multiple occasions she let me know how "crazy" her elderly roommate was. Upon going through her things after her passing, I found that my mom had squirreled away the roommate's lotion in the back of her nightstand drawer. I can only guess at my mom's delight in getting back at her roommate by hiding the lotion.

On April 29, 2020, we were granted special exception to enter the nursing home as my mom was considered end of life. For the next two days my spouse and my two children and I spent hours upon end at her bedside. She passed away a little after midnight on May the first, 2020.

We were blessed that her dementia never exceeded the point of her knowing who we were. God is so very good – many of my prayers were answered, even though they were answered in an unexpected way, for only a short amount of time. Although not normal, I feel that the declining mental road of dementia caused my mother's mental clarity in regard to our relationship. It has once again shown me that God truly does take beauty from ashes. (Isaiah 61:3) Dementia truly took a mother but gave me my mom.

Submitted by Laura H.

"Therefore if anyone is in Christ, he is a new creature; the old things passed away; behold, new things have come." 2 Corinthians 5:17 NASB1995 "Do not call to mind the former things, Or ponder things of the past. "Behold, I will do something new, Now it will spring forth; Will you not be aware of it? I will even make a roadway in the wilderness, Rivers in the desert." Isaiah 43:18-19 NASB 1995

"The Spirit of the Lord God is upon me, Because the Lord has anointed me To bring good news to the afflicted; He has sent me to bind up the brokenhearted, To proclaim liberty to captives And freedom to prisoners; Isaiah 61:1 NASB1995

NOTES:

Reva McCubbins was the most kindhearted, loving woman on earth. To her family, she was absolutely perfect. She was so full of life and would light up a room as soon as she walked in. She loved her husband, her kids, grandkids, and great grandkids more than life itself; honestly, she loved everyone she met. She always made you feel like she had been waiting to see you all day and when she finally saw you her day was complete. Every time she saw you, no matter who you were, she would "beat" you on your back as soon as you got close enough for her to reach you. She loved to love and by just being close to her you could feel how much she loved you.

Reva was so energetic and no matter if it was five o'clock in the morning or midnight, she was always ready to whistle, dance and laugh. She was so happy with everything life had to offer. She would love talking about and trying the latest trends going around except jeans with holes and rips in them. She hated ripped jeans and no matter if she had seen you wear them a million times, she would tell you each time about how much she did not like them.

The disease slowly at first, then aggressively took her from her family and friends. She did not recognize herself as a wife, mother, grandmother, or great grandmother. She became a walking shell of a person that was always looking for "home", constantly saying "I want to go home" or "Take me home". One day she was able to go home, and her mind was finally at peace.

Reva may have passed on, and we miss her terribly every day, but her memories will always live within us.

Submitted by Dina L.

"Consider it all joy, my brethren, when you encounter various trials, knowing that the testing of your faith produces endurance. And let endurance have its perfect result, so that you may be perfect and complete, lacking in nothing." James 1:2-4 NASB 1995

"And do not be conformed to this world, but be transformed by the renewing of your mind, so that you may prove what the will of God is, that which is good and acceptable and perfect." Romans 12:2 NASB

"And He who sits on the throne said, "Behold, I am making all things new." And He said, "Write, for these words are faithful and true." Revelation 21:5 NASB1995

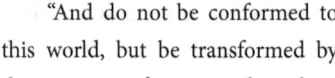 **NOTES:**

_____

_____

_____

_____

_____

_____

_____

_____

CHAPTER TWO

LOVE

When asked to write my story for the book called, "Don't Forget Me" my mind instantly thought of memory. Memory is a powerful blessing that God has blessed us with, and we take it for granted every day until we see a loved one loose it. My story begins about my wife, Nita, who I was married to for 45 years. We endured a journey with one of the most devastating diseases called Primary Progressive Aphasia, a cousin to dementia and all others that effect the memory. When I married this gal, we were both nineteen years old. Nita was one of the most brilliant people I had ever seen. I remember in bible college she strived to make the Dean's list every semester and did. She ranked in the top 50 of all students that included all the colleges across America. I bought the book that had them all listed, and her name is in it. I was so proud of her for such an achievement. There was nothing that she couldn't do. She could sew anything. She worked on her own computer, worked as a nurse for many years and finally leaving that to run her own successful business doing screen printing on shirts. This was about the time I noticed something wasn't right because she became confused and agitated. This was not Nita. I took her to our family doctor and explained to them her problem. From there she was sent to Louisville for further diagnosis. This was when we she was diagnosed with Primary Progressive Aphasia. As time progressed, she developed even more symptoms such as speech problems that included difficulty forming words and frequent pausing in her words. She began having problems with comprehension. She eventually became like an elementary student and couldn't spell some of the simplest words. As she advanced deeper into this consuming disease it was like quicksand and every day, I watched her sink deeper and deeper with no way to save her. It was the most devastating disease I had ever seen. She no longer remembered our anniversary and forgot who I was. After 45 years all the history we built together was gone! She eventually plunged deeper into this disease and became bed ridden. She stopped eating, barely sipped water, and required 24/7 care. Finally, Hosparus came to my home. They are a fantastic organization. I did not work for several weeks because I felt the need to stay home and be by her side even though she didn't know me, because I knew her, and she would have done the same thing for me. The journey with this disease was tough but my love for her followed her to the end because that's what we do for our loved ones. Every morning when I got up the first thing I would do was walk into Nita's room not knowing if it would be our last day together. It was the hardest thing I ever faced in my 63 years of life. I know and believe that God promised better days for her and all of us who believe and put our faith in Him only. Jesus said in John 10:10, " the thief comes only to steal and kill and destroy; I came

so they would have life and have it more abundantly". That speaks volumes to me. Even though this disease, this thief, has stolen everything from me including the life of my wife, I believe there is hope in the end. If you are currently on the same journey, please find the hope that's in Christ. It's all that's left and remember to thank God for your memory.

Submitted by Bo S.

"He who finds a wife finds a good thing and obtains favor from the Lord." Proverbs 18:22 NASB1995

"House and wealth are an inheritance from fathers, but a prudent wife is from the Lord." Proverbs 19:14 NASB1995

"An excellent wife, who can find? For her worth is far above jewels. The heart of her husband trusts in her, And he will have no lack of gain." Proverbs 31:10-11 NASB1995

NOTES:

_____

_____

_____

_____

_____

_____

_____

_____

_____

_____

_____

_____

_____

_____

_____

_____

Alzheimer's is a very cruel disease and affects so many families. As the spouse of an Alzheimer's patient, you suffer emotional pain that no one realizes, and you try to pretend that all is well!

My husband was a farmer and such a hard-working man. He was so much fun, very social and loved joking around with people. We met in 1972 on a Sunday afternoon, fell in love quickly, and married six months later. We had a great marriage! Working together on the farm and raising three wonderful children was the best life!

The signs of Alzheimer's for Gene were gradual. He was in his late sixties when I began to see signs that something was not quite right. At first, I was in denial and tried to make excuses for some of the things that were happening, but eventually I realized it was getting worse instead of better.

For several years Gene often repeated the same conversations over and over, lost many things and blamed it on one of us and seemed very confused at times, but he was still able to do many things around the house and farm. He knew that me, the children, and the grandchildren were familiar to him, but did not always know our names or our connection.

As the disease continued to progress, one of the hardest things for me was that I no longer had a spouse, it seemed. Even though his body was present, he was not the same vibrant person that I could go to for strength. I had to become the strong one making all the decisions even with his life and health. There was no longer intimacy because I no longer felt like a spouse, but a caretaker. It was a stressful and emotional time.

Fortunately, Gene never became bedfast until the last few weeks. His appetite diminished, so he ate very little and eventually he became so weak. My children, grandchildren and I were able to love him and take care of him at home until his death. We were so thankful for that. He was a special man and I loved him through it all.

Your wife, Nancy

Submitted by Nancy H.

"If I have the gift of prophecy, and know all mysteries and all knowledge; and if I have all faith, so as to remove mountains, but do not have love, I am nothing." 1 Corinthians 13:2 NASB1995

"Love is patient, love is kind and is not jealous; love does not brag and is not arrogant, does not act unbecomingly; it does not seek its own, is not provoked, does not take into account a wrong suffered, does not rejoice in unrighteousness, but rejoices with the truth;" 1 Corinthians 13:4-6 NASB1995

"Beloved, if God so loved us, we also ought to love one another." 1 John 4:11 NASB1995

NOTES:

To Donnie,

This terrible disease is so unforgiving. You didn't ever think you would ever have to deal with this in our younger years. Now, I begin to understand the marriage vow, "In sickness and in health, till death do us part". We used to have a lot of heated conversations, now there are none. He can't relate to almost any topic.

Donnie, you were the rock of our family, you refused to pay someone to do a job that you knew you could learn and do yourself. You were a mechanic at heart but also taught yourself to construct buildings, even wired your dad's new garage.

You always did all the driving, but now I do it since you have no idea where you are or where you're going. You now also want my opinion on a lot of things. I know it was hard for you to give up driving, but you handled it well. You were a top-notch mechanic. You loved collecting old cars and were able to work on them too. As this disease has progressed, you no longer know why or how to do what you could have once done with your eyes closed.

You had taught our kids and grandkids a lot about a vehicle maintenance. You instilled a good work ethic in all your family.

You never were one to say "I'm sorry" before this awful disease. Now we hear it all the time. It was also hard for you to tell anyone you loved them, but we knew by some of the things you did, it was obvious.

I thank God, that you still know a few of our names, or at least recognize our faces but can't say the name out loud.

You loved your kids, me, and the grandkids so much. Your face lights up, even still, whenever they are around. You have told me you love me more in the last 5 years than in the last 56 years, before this hit our family.

Yes, we've been married for 61 years now, and you never learned how to say "I love you" in the spring, summer and fall of our lives. Now that we our in the final days of the winter of our lives, you say it all the time, and this is not your fault, it happens with a lot of people. None of us are perfect.

God willing, you will be around for us for many more years. You were not always the nicest person at times, but who is? The winter of your life is here now.

Donnie, I love you so much, Mary Etta

Submitted by Mary Etta B.

"But now faith, hope, love, abide these three; but the greatest of these is love." 1 Corinthians 13:13 NASB1995

"Beyond all these things put on love, which is the perfect bond of unity." Colossians 3:14 NASB1995

"And if I give all my possessions to feed the poor, and if I surrender my body to be burned, but do not have love, it profits me nothing." 1 Corinthians 13:3 NASB1995

NOTES:

CHAPTER THREE

GENTLENESS

When I was 5, my grandfather passed away and we had to move in with my grandmother to help take care of her. She wasn't fully into her dementia stages yet, but we knew she would be lonely. She was very independent, and a good homemaker. She liked for things to be kept neat and tidy. One of the things she loved was making breakfast for all her grandkids on Sunday mornings. Mamaw always had a big breakfast for us, and nobody made it as good as she did. Over time, I noticed that things started to change. Some stuff wasn't cooked like it had always been. She would leave the oven and the stove on. She would leave things half cooked in the microwave. Something she once took pride in was no longer the same. It wasn't long after that she was placed into long term care and began to forget more than just breakfast. February 9th, 2019, the Lord called her home to be with Papaw again, and to take away her pain and clear her mind.

Submitted by Taylor G.

"Blessed are the merciful, for they shall receive mercy." Matthew Matthew 5:7 NASB1995

"Do not withhold good from those to whom it is due, when it is in your power to do it." Proverbs 3:27 NASB1995

"Be kind to one another, tender-hearted, forgiving each other, just as God in Christ also has forgiven you." Ephesians 4:32 NASB1995

NOTES:

REMEMBERING

Charles C.

You were my best friend
Who lived across the street,
Then you moved away
And wrote me a letter I never read
You remembered who I was

You were my best friend
We were seldom apart
We played, we sang
I sat by your side during recovery
You moved away
You remembered who I was

You were my best shipmate
We laughed, we cried
We sailed the seas and explored the ruins
You returned home
You remembered who I was

You were my mother
Watching me blossom
We Raised a family
You wept when we moved
You remembered who I was
You cared for your husband
Until his time came to an end

Relocating with us
To finish your days
Until you couldn't remember, who I was

Submitted by Charles C.

"Blessed are the gentle, for they shall inherit the earth." Matthew 5:5 NASB1995

"Do not let kindness and truth leave you; Bind them around your neck, Write them on the tablet of your heart." Proverbs 3:3 NASB1995

"So, as those who have been chosen of God, holy and beloved, put on a heart of compassion, kindness, humility, gentleness and patience;" Colossians 3:12 NASB1995

NOTES:

_____

_____

_____
_____
_____
_____
_____

Shop

Ever since I was about fourteen years old, helping clean up the shop was one of my first jobs and kind of a rite of passage in our family. We all had our turns helping out or cleaning up DeeDee's shop. Cleaning those floors that never seemed to come all the way clean, and the smell of oil and smoke filled the air. Sundays were the days I'd come out to do my duties but also spend time with DeeDee. We'd always have our little chats when we first got there, he'd ask about my week, and jokingly asked what trouble I'd been into lately. I'd always ask how he was and how he was doing, being an old man and all. One of my most prominent memories was when I'd be in the middle of cleaning, he'd come find me and give me a hand full of peppermints; the ones he'd taken from church just hours before. He'd say here's something sweet for my sweet girl. That's a memory that will never fade.

During my teenage years, on Sundays I'd go out to Boston Road, walk myself up to the barn and find the old man underneath an old car, wearing his works clothes and grease covered hands. He'd already have a car picked out for me to get cleaned up. He'd help me set up out of the washroom by the barn. After every wash we'd take them for a drive. We had our usual route that we took out by the airport. He claimed it was to get it good and dry, but I loved those silent drives, just feeling the wind and sun hit my face. Sometimes he would let me drive if the car had an automatic transmission.

He attempted to teach me how to drive a stick, which was him telling me to get in, start it up and try to not to run in to stuff. I never got it down. However, he did successfully teach me how to start up one of the oldies by adding fuel directly into the carburetor. Works every time.

Submitted by Whitney H.

"Treat others the same way you want them to treat you." Luke 6:31 NASB1995

"Let your speech always be with grace, as though seasoned with salt, so that you will know how you should respond to each person." Colossians 4:6 NASB1995

"With all humility and gentleness, with patience, showing tolerance for one another in love," Ephesians 4:2 NASB1995

NOTES:

_____

_____

_____

_____

_____

_____

_____

_____

_____

CHAPTER FOUR

FAITHFULNESS

How do you summarize the life of your favorite person in the world? Do you talk about the weeks you spent with her in the summer as a kid, when you would take walks to the creek, and she would force you to take embarrassing pictures in front of her favorite flowers? What about the evenings you would make special trips to Dairy Queen to get blueberry milkshakes, or when she would let you help make brownies? You would struggle to stir the thick batter but somehow, she would effortlessly whip that spoon around the bowl to give it one final stir. Or do you talk about her love for gospel music, and how she always did chores around the house while singing "The Old Rugged Cross" and "What A Day That Will Be" and "Because He Lives"? Or do you talk about how she never met a stranger, and how she would talk to anyone who would listen, making her way around church pews and her favorite Mexican restaurant, and leaving voicemails that lasted no less than 2-3 minutes? Or do you talk about her silly jokes and her little cartoon drawings on any scrap piece of paper that was lying around? Maybe you talk about her big, wonderful meals, especially at Thanksgiving and Christmas, and her perfect homemade biscuits (yes, she let us help with those too). You could also talk about her love for the little things, her cats she would always accumulate outside, her hummingbirds, her flowers, and bushes in her yard, sending cards in the mail, sometimes multiple cards because she couldn't pick just one. Or do you talk about how, when it was time for you to leave, she would somehow wrap you up in conversations for at least another 30 minutes on your way out the door? No matter how cold it was outside, she would always stand in her front yard with Papaw and wave goodbye with both arms up above her head.

One thing I know for sure, is that she loved me. She loved me so deeply, in such a way that only a grandmother can. She always made me feel so special. Even as an adult, I still had that same feeling around her as I did when I was little.

Though her final years were devastated by Alzheimer's/dementia, and I think it had been a couple years since she truly knew who I was, I never forgot her. It just doesn't feel right living in a world where she no longer lives too. But there is comfort in the Lord and knowing that she is no longer struggling. She's finally made it to where she's longed for so long to be, with her Lord and Savior Jesus Christ.

"I have fought the good fight, I have finished the race, I have kept the faith. Now there is in store for me the crown of righteousness, which the Lord, the righteous Judge, will award to me on that day." 2 Timothy 4:7-8

She was the best Nanny I could've ever asked for.

Submitted by Breanna A.

"Speaking to one another in psalms and hymns and spiritual songs, singing and making melody with your heart to the Lord;" Ephesians 5:19 NASB1995

"I have fought the good fight, I have finished the course, I have kept the faith; in the future there is laid up for me the crown of righteousness, which the Lord, the righteous Judge, will award to me on that day; and not only to me, but also to all who have loved His appearing." 2 Timothy 4:7-8 NASB1995

"O satisfy us in the morning with Your lovingkindness, That we may sing for joy and be glad all our days." Psalms Psalms 90:14 NASB1995

NOTES:

_____

_____

_____

_____

_____

_____

_____

_____

_____

_____

_____

_____

_____

_____

_____

_____

Jenny

This is the story of Jenny before dementia took her at the age of 64. She had a stroke at the age of 50 and recovered completely but six years later started showing signs that something wasn't quite right. After an examination and countless tests, she was diagnosed, and it went from there.

She was a woman loved by many. She was the 13th of 14 children. She had a servant's heart and cared for many family members in our home from time to time as they were battling cancer or an automobile accident or just needed a place to stay for a while. Jenny loved her Louisville Cardinals and cheered them on many times right there in her family room. She was a fantastic cook and was well known for her meatloaf and mashed potatoes.

Jenny was married to the love of her life, John, for forty-eight years. She called him "my honey". Jenny and John had four children. Jenny loved to sing and even when she could no longer communicate, when she went to church, she would sing along with the songs. When she first gave her heart to the Lord, she couldn't control her excitement and even prayed that God would calm her down. She never missed a sporting event that her children were involved in. When grandchildren came along, she was so in love with them and called them her "cootsie bugs".

Once her children were grown, she went to work for Gibson Greeting Cards and set up displays in stores for Kroger in Shively to Kroger in Valley Station. She loved to shop and was dubbed the "Layaway Queen of Louisville" as she traveled from one end of Dixie

Highway to the other stopping on her lunch at either Fashion Shop, K-Mart or Value City on the way.

Submitted by Theresa K.

"I will give thanks to You, O Lord my God, with all my heart, And will glorify Your name forever." Psalms 86:12 NASB1995

"Bear one another's burdens, and thereby fulfill the law of Christ." Galatians 6:10 NASB1995

"Let us not lose heart in doing good, for in due time we will reap if we do not grow weary." Galatians 6:2 NASB1995

NOTES:

_____

_____

_____

_____

_____

_____

_____

_____

I have many memories of times together with my grandpa. One of the memories I have of DeeDee is tagging along while he played golf with his buddies when I was a kid and later into life. We both enjoyed playing the game together and it allowed me to spend a lot of time with him. That time helped him to teach me many things, not just about golf but other things as well. Like when we were playing in the springtime and he had a runny nose, he proceeded to eat some grass to help his immunity, half an hour later no runny nose. That crazy grandpa hack actually worked. That kinda taught me to look at things differently and think outside the box.

I've also worked with him at the family mower dealership since I was twelve, I'm now thirty-seven. I remember talking to a long-time customer of DeeDee's in my mid twenty's, he said he always comes back because Don stands behind what he sells. I later saw examples of him doing just that when he had no obligation to do so. That is something I'll never forget, and it made me realize that he was an honest, honorable man.

We've been dealing with with his decline for a few years now. I remember years back when he was of sound mind jokingly saying "Boy, I've forgot more than you'll ever know." That statement rings truer every day. I try to remember all the good memories and do what I can to make him smile and laugh. Although he doesn't remember eating the grass to stop his runny nose, or even playing golf for that matter, what he has taught me over the years I will both cherish and appreciate.

Submitted by Damien U.

"And without faith it is impossible to please Him, for he who comes to God must believe that He is and that He is a rewarder of those who seek Him." Hebrews 11:6 NASB1995

"He who pursues righteousness and loyalty Finds life, righteousness and honor." Proverbs 21:21 NASB1995

"Delight yourself in the LORD; And He will give you the desires of your heart. Commit your way to the LORD, Trust also in Him, and He will do it." Psalms Psalms 37:4-5 NASB

NOTES:

_____

_____

_____

_____

_____

_____

_____

_____

_____

_____

CHAPTER FIVE

MOTHERS

March 8, 1934, our Momma was born into the world. Alzheimer's took her from us at the young age of seventy-eight. Beauty, elegance, baker, and faithful are just some of the words that described her.

She was married to the love of her life until a freak sledding accident took his life. At the age of thirty-three she found herself a single mother of three young children. She owned a local, thriving women's dress shop. Quickly it became quite the hotspot for fashion, women, and the go-to for men at Christmas time.

On snowy, winter days and nights our home was filled with friends, laughter and food. Card games were played while wet, snowy clothes ran continuously in a hot dryer for trip after trip of sledding in the nearby field. Momma made sure her home was always open, warm, and welcoming.

She was a teacher, not in education but in morals, life, right and wrong. When Ricky bought his first car, she taught him a lesson of tough love. He remembers her teaching him that bills came before you do anything else. She also taught that family comes first. Having her whole family together on Christmas morning was a favorite of hers through the years.

Baking and Momma were synonymous. From yeast rolls to pastries, she was most comfortable in the kitchen. This was passed down to Rhonda. Baking for family is a "sweet" tradition passed down to several in the family.

Saundra remembers her always being dressed to the nines, perfectly put together. Whether it was to church, where her faith was deep, or a community event, she had the shoes that matched the lipstick that matched the dress.

Momma, Grandma, sister, no matter who she was to whom, she was loved, and she's missed.

Submitted by Emily J., Rhonda N., Saundra S., & Rick W.

"Charm is deceitful and beauty is vain, But a woman who fears the Lord, she shall be praised." Proverbs 31:30 NASB1995

"She is not afraid of the snow for her household, For all her household are clothed with scarlet." Proverbs 31:21 NASB1995

"She opens her mouth in wisdom, And the teaching of kindness is on her tongue." Proverbs 31:26 NASB1995

NOTES:

_____

_____

_____

_____

_____

_____

_____

_____

Our Mother, Twila, was born the eighth of ten children during the depression years. She was taught to cook for a large family and work hard on the farm. She continued that work ethic throughout her ninety years of life. She married at the age of twenty, and she and her husband raised six children on the farm, teaching them the same work ethic she was taught as a child. As a young wife and mother, she worked hard to help provide for the family. She milked cows, planted, and harvested a big garden every year, raised chickens, and pumped water from the well as there was no running water in the house for several years. If you came to visit in her home, she always made sure you had something to eat before you left or something to take with you. It is no surprise that as her children grew, she went to work as a cook and dietary supervisor at the local nursing home. She spent twenty-six years working at the same home she would later spend the last nine months of her life. She was a mother that attended every school event, ballgame, and community activity her children were involved in. She later did the same with her ten grandchildren. She was even known to play a mean game of softball herself, as well as a tough game of UNO in her later years. Family was the most important thing in her life and along with that was the importance of education. She was the first of her family to graduate high school and made sure all her children did the same. She was also extremely proud of the educational accomplishments of her ten grandchildren. Each also continued their education beyond high school, with two of them receiving their PHD's.

Submitted by Darlene C.

"She rises also while it is still night And gives food to her household And portions to her maidens." Proverbs 31:15 NASB1995

"She girds herself with strength And makes her arms strong." Proverbs 31:17 NASB1995

"She senses that her gain is good; Her lamp does not go out at night." Proverbs 31:18 NASB1995

NOTES:

_____

_____

_____

_____

_____

_____

_____

_____

_____

_____

_____

_____

_____

Never in million years, did I think I would be writing this. Never in a million years, did I think she would be one of the statistics. Never in a million years, would I have to worry that she would forget who I was – her oldest daughter. Never in a million years, would I cry the tears I have because I cannot help her. I cannot help her to remember. I cannot help her to feel safe. She is trapped and cannot escape. I cannot help her to remember what I remember – she's my momma.

My memories float back to those days as a child when she was cooking bacon and pancakes for supper. Best supper ever. My sister and I never had store-bought clothes. Momma was an incredible seamstress. She would lay us down on the floor on a piece of newspaper and trace our bodies. This would become the pattern for many a dress. Every, and I mean every Christmas and Easter, a special dress was made for my sister and I that matched my momma. She would even make daddy a matching tie. Even our Barbie dolls had our matching outfits. Momma could just look and sew, and it was magic. The memories of Midnight Mass and her attending our school functions have played an important part of my journey as a mom. I don't know that she will ever be able to understand my love for her.

Memories are treasured moments. Those moments that took place so long ago have become the journey. How long the journey continues, only the good Lord knows. I hate this disease. I don't look towards the future any longer. I only take the day that has been given to me. A day that she still remembers me. Another day, that I can say "Don't Forget Me".

Submitted by Deanna "DeDe" C

"She looks for wool and flax And works with her hands in delight." Proverbs 31:13 NASB1995

"She makes coverings for herself; Her clothing is fine linen and purple." Proverbs 31:22 NASB1995

"She looks well to the ways of her household, And does not eat the bread of idleness." Proverbs 31:27 NASB1995

NOTES:

_____

_____

_____

_____

_____

_____

_____

_____

_____

_____

CHAPTER SIX

FATHERS

On a cold, dark night on December 13, 1982, Dad stopped to help a stranded motorist, not knowing that this one decision would change his life forever. While helping the other motorist, a drunk driver struck the vehicle in the rear, pinning Dad between two of the vehicles. As a result of the accident, he lost one leg and the other was badly broken and was never quite the same. Despite his injuries, Dad was able to rehabilitate with the help of a prosthetic leg and months of therapy. After several months, he returned to work, working as a timekeeper for the state highway department. In 1987, he bought a farm and spent the next twenty plus years working the farm, raising crops, cutting hay, mowing fields, raising hogs, cattle, chickens, ducks, and geese. In addition to working a public job and farming, Dad also dedicated countless hours working as a deacon in his church which included visiting the sick, the shut-ins, and helping those in need. He loved spending time with family and friends. Dad, known as Donnie by family and friends, had eight siblings and many nieces, nephews, and cousins. In addition to that, he had five children, fifteen grandchildren and ten great-grandchildren before the time of his death. Big crowds of family members were never uncommon. He loved to host large barn parties and family reunions and gatherings on the farm. He managed to stay active and busy most of the time. In 2009, he sold his cattle and started leasing the farm to others for cropping. Dad still managed to stay active with other farm upkeep chores, mowing and church work. In early 2015 at the age of seventy-two, he began to slow down and seemed to lose interest in things that kept him active and motivated before. Through a series of events, we noticed that Dad wasn't the same as he had been before. He refused to wear his prosthetic leg which confined him to a wheelchair. He was eventually diagnosed with Alzheimer's disease. Because of this horrible disease, Dad seemed to stop living, years before he died. We lost the man we knew several times over before he passed and then we lost him one last time. Often while being one of Dad's caregivers, I struggled with many things, especially in assisting with frequent bathroom visits and bathing. I tried to do these things in a way to allow him to maintain his dignity while maintaining mine as well. During the caregiving, I would often struggle to remember the man he was before. Dad passed June 16, 2020, and we buried him the day before Father's Day that year. Soon after his death, the memories of the man before the disease came flooding back in. It was almost overwhelming yet bittersweet. I am so thankful for those memories and the man he was because that made me the man I am.

Submitted by Dean P.

"Grandchildren are the crown of old men, And the glory of sons is their fathers." Proverbs 17:6 NASB1995

"Let no one seek his own good, but that of his neighbor." 1 Corinthians 10:24 NASB1995

"Yet those who wait for the Lord Will gain new strength; They will mount up with wings like eagles, They will run and not get tired, They will walk and not become weary." Isaiah 40:31 NASB1995

NOTES:

_____

_____

_____

_____

_____

_____

_____

_____

_____

_____

_____

_____

_____

_____

_____

_____

_____

_____

_____

_____

_____

_____

_____

_____

_____

_____

_____

Daddy (His working hands)

One of my fondest memories of my daddy, Donnie, was that he was always one of the strongest, smartest men I had ever known. As a child, I remember that he worked all the time. He started his own business at the young age of twenty-four, with our momma, and she was always by his side. They had a very successful business in the farm machinery world and later in the lawn equipment business for over fifty years.

As a child, I wanted to be in the garage watching him work his magic. He would figure out almost anything. As a young child, I was very impressed by his drive. I loved being by his side getting dirty. I thought he was the smartest, wittiest, most talented man I had ever known. He could figure out how to make anything work. He would take things completely apart, just to see how it worked. He had his own way of fixing things and figuring out how make things work. I have used what I learned from him to fix things throughout my life. Another important lesson that I learned is to never give up until the job is done. He wouldn't quit until the job was complete. He instilled, in us kids, that if you want something, you must work hard and earn it, no free hand-outs. You should save enough for it and then, you could buy it.

He was so strong, and even at the age of 82, he still amazes me with his strength. He doesn't give up even though he gets confused and moves a little slower.

It is disheartening to see the uncertainty in his speech, the stuttering to find his words, and the lost looks. Often, he appears confused at where he is and how he or things got where they are.

Today, this man, that I had once put on a pedestal, is now unable to follow the smallest task. We give him one task at a time to minimize confusion and frustration while giving him constant supervision repeating that one task over and over.

He has been unable to call me by my name for nearly two years. I think he sees me as a co-worker. Since developing dementia, he has been more complimentary, loving, and caring. His words are now kinder than they once were. This man recently has told me he loves me, and how proud he is of me. Until now, I had never heard those words from his mouth. He says he is just amazed at the hard work I do and compliments me daily. I had waited fifty-eight years to hear these words, it seems this disease does have its pros, at least that is how I choose to look at it.

Daddy seems to be at his best when he is around his great grandkids. He will, for a few seconds, speak in plain sentences to them. At those times, its like there is nothing wrong with him, unfortunately, this doesn't last very long. It gives me moments of comfort to see the "old" him, which makes me smile and happy inside.

I feel blessed every day to be working side by side with him but realizing that we are losing him a little more each day. Sometimes that knowledge is unbearable. As a family, we try our best to keep things light to protect him or us, just not sure who we are protecting. We try not to concentrate on how fast he is "slowly slipping away", but to absorb every second we can with him. As my sister states it best, "One day at a time".

It is hard on all who love him, realizing that this man who once was so full of energy and life, is slipping away daily. It's like a very slow, painful goodbye. He is now totally dependent on others for constant care and guidance.

He sees me as someone who picks him up and takes him to work almost every day, to his very own business, that he can no longer run himself due to this awful disease that is stealing our daddy from us. He has called me many names due to not being able to remember my real name. Some of the names are not always appropriate, but I answer to them all, to honor what little bit of pride he has left in himself. Never in a million years did I ever think how much I would need to hear my name called by my daddy. It is completely heart breaking and devastating at times. For him to just remember that I am his daughter, would be a huge blessing right now but will never be.

I find myself speaking to him as if talking to one of my young grandsons, speaking slowly and clearly, with that "one task at a time" rule. I constantly repeat everything, trying my best not to get frustrated and praying daily for strength to stay patient with my daddy. Lord knows, its a daily challenge, for us all.

I had prayed so hard, that my wonderful Daddy, would not forget me. However, I am thankful that he still recognizes me as someone he loves and seems to enjoy working with daily. Until we can no long do this together, I will absorb and cherish ever second with My Daddy.

I Love You Always Daddy
Your daughter, Donetta

Submitted by Donetta H.

A good name is to be more desired than great wealth, Favor is better than silver and gold." Proverbs 22:1 NASB1995

"Do you see a man skilled in his work? He will stand before kings; He will not stand before obscure men." Proverbs 22:29 NASB1995

"Many a man proclaims his own loyalty, But who can find a trustworthy man?" Proverbs 20:6 NASB1995

NOTES:

_____

_____

_____

_____

_____

_____

_____

_____

_____

_____

_____

_____

_____

Joe was a light-complexed, muscular, medium, deep-voice man, that was not loud, but matter of fact. We always teased Daddy, that his hands felt like sandpaper, from the work he did. When I close my eyes, and breathe in, I can get a hint of that Old Spice, he always wore. He survived the great flood of 1936, the year he was born. He came into this world a fighter and that is how he left it! Joe always stood for the right thing. He believed in the word truth and that is what he taught his daughters. Joe was an athlete who played all sports. He once scored fifty-three points in a high school basketball game! He was Valedictorian of his class, and attended Xavier University in Louisiana, where he played football and basketball. Joe was also a Medic in the Army; Yakama was his favorite place to talk about!

Joe was married to his high school sweetheart, Rosie, and they had two daughters, Shonna, and Kim. He was a hard worker, and family was everything to him. He coached little league sports; Joe coached like he played, HARD! His teams won championships and produced some great high school and college athletes. Joe was a soft-spoken man, but what he said, he meant. He had a style about himself, when he stepped into the room, you noticed his cool walk, and his style of dress. Joe's trademark was his love of hats, he was never caught without one.

Joe was affectionally known, of course, as Daddy, Jo-o-o-e, as my mom would drag out, Da, Joe D., and Head. He answered to all. Joe was a simple man and wanted the best for everyone he encountered.

Submitted by Shonna S.

"Iron sharpens iron, So one man sharpens another." Proverbs 27:17 NASB1995

"Open your mouth for the mute, For the rights of all the unfortunate. Open your mouth, judge righteously, And defend the rights of the afflicted and needy." Proverbs 31:8-9 NASB1995

"Teach me Your way, O Lord; I will walk in Your truth; Unite my heart to fear Your name." Psalms 86:11 NASB1995

NOTES:

_____

_____

_____

_____

_____

_____

_____

_____

_____

_____

_____

CHAPTER SEVEN

PATIENCE

Dementia, a word I cringe to hear. Did you know the synonym for Dementia, is madness? I know my Grandpa Chuck, my mom's dad, as he got much older, was diagnosed with a severe case of Dementia. It was so bad, that they had to call the police one day. He was getting upset and lashing out

that a stranger was in their apartment. It was a hired lady that came in to help Grandma. But this specific day Grandpa didn't remember her. After that incident, he was forced to move into a nursing home and Grandma then decided to pack up her things and go with him. Things didn't get better there. They kept him strapped down to a bed, so he wouldn't hurt himself or others. There was one person her never forgot, the love of his life, my grandma, Edna.

Fast forward to now, 2021. A little over a year ago, was that one phone call when you know something isn't right. I was on the phone with my mom, and we were having one of our normal one to two-hour conversations. But this one was different. In the middle of our conversation, she asked me about a topic we had already talked about in detail. It was like we hadn't even talked about it. We talked about it again and finished our conversation. Each phone call seemed to be about the same, off and on memory loss conversations. All of us that would talk to her began noticing it here and there. My sisters and I talked and agreed that mom needed to see a doctor and see if something could be done and catch it early.

One day, out of the blue, she calls extremely upset, explaining how she got lost for two hours driving the country roads around her house. She couldn't find her way home from running some errands. Leaving the bank to head home, she ran into a detour. As she proceeded towards home, she began realizing she wasn't sure where she was. Nothing was looking right. She found herself lost on roads that were once familiar to her. She said she tried to use her dashboard map in her Expedition. She couldn't get it to work, no matter what buttons she pushed. Even though it works fine now. She tried to find her map app on her phone and couldn't find it or figure out where it was on the screen. After driving around for a bit, extremely upset, crying, and feeling somewhat embarrassed she came upon a little gas station mart and asked for directions. She got the directions and made it back home safely. When she got there, she settled in and tried to recall everything that happened. When she had called, I asked her why she didn't call me, or one of my sisters so that maybe one of us could have helped calm her and given her directions home. She said, at the time that it was all happening, she couldn't even think of who to call. She now has all of us daughters and a few other people on an emergency contact list on her phone.

She has been to the Doctor. She was diagnosed with early-onset Dementia and prescribed some medication. The first medication didn't do very well and had some side effects. They then prescribed her something else, and she seems to be doing a lot better. Don't get me wrong, the medication isn't a cure, but it does help with some clarity and short-term memory. Mom is still in there and still remembers a lot. But, during the time her memory was suffering before diagnosis, she has had a hard time recalling things from then.

Our mom is 65 years young. She has a couple of older siblings that haven't been affected by this, and a younger sibling still living also, that isn't showing signs. It's just scary. Who does it affect next?

Will it be me? Will I recognize it happening? Will I become lost inside, and lose my memory? It seems to be genetic, so where will it show next?

It has scared me enough but inspired me again, to start writing more things down, hand-written journals, pictures, and going to do more scrapbooking as well. One day I may not remember how to turn on a computer, to access it all. And having handwritten memories and mementos may still be the way to go.

Submitted by Jennifer C.

"And not only this, but we also exult in our tribulations, knowing that tribulation brings about perseverance; and perseverance, proven character; and proven character, hope;"Romans 5:3-4 NASB1995

"Wait for the Lord; Be strong and let your heart take courage; Yes, wait for the Lord." Psalms 27:14 NASB1995

"But if we hope for what we do not see, with perseverance we wait eagerly for it." Romans 8:25 NASB1995

(Right to Left & Front Geri, "Mom" Debbie, Jennifer, Kristi)

NOTES:

Ruth was a loving and caring wife and mother before dementia took her from us at the age of sixty-seven in 2005. Although she physically gave birth to only six children, she was the adopted mother to all the children on Edith Road. Everyone, adults, and children, would love to sit on the front porch with Ruth and share stories or talk about the current events of the world or the simpler life of living on the hill. She was the fun one, playing kick ball with all the kids in the court, being the roller for both teams, helping to catch lightning bugs or starting water balloon fights. The list goes on. She would always give her time to anyone who needed it, including volunteering at the grade school. She was an avid fan of all sports and enjoyed watching her children and later her beloved grandchildren participate in an array of sports. Dementia may have robbed Ruth of her physical abilities for the last ten years of her life, but it wasn't able to rob her of the love everyone had for her, and it couldn't take away all the wonderful memories that she was able to leave behind.

Submitted by Theresa K.

"My mouth is filled with Your praise And with Your glory all day long." Psalms 71:8 NASB1995

"Let your light shine before men in such a way that they may see your good works, and glorify your Father who is in heaven." Matthew 5:16 NASB1995

"Do you not know that those who run in a race all run, but only one

receives the prize? Run in such a way that you may win. Everyone who competes in the games exercises self-control in all things. They then do it to receive a perishable wreath, but we an imperishable."
1Corinthians 9:24-25 NASB1995

NOTES:

_____

_____

_____

_____

_____

_____

_____

_____

_____

_____

_____

_____

_____

_____

_____

_____

_____

_____

_____

When I think about Donald "Donnie", or as I call him, Deedee, I instantly smile. Growing up as a kid he was the best grandpa, and had all the cool toys, like a boat, a jet ski, a snowmobile, go carts, and he would play along with us too. However, my most treasured memories are of the times I worked side by side with him at his shop. He taught me so many things like how to change tires, plug them on my own, and service my own vehicle. I have put shingles on a roof, blacktopped the parking lots, and have become the queen of rigging something up. He taught me that, even as a female, there wasn't anything I couldn't do. He is by far one of the strongest, smartest, and funniest people I have ever known. When his friends would come into the shop, and he would brag on some of the things I was doing, it would fill my heart with so much pride. Watching that light inside him slowly disappear is truly heart breaking. I never knew how much I would miss hearing him call me Kelli. Most days now he doesn't know who I am and cannot recall all the memories we have made. I, on the other hand, think of those times more now than I ever have. I will forever feel blessed for the days I was his right

hand (wo)man. One lesson he taught me that I use in every single day of my life is "If you take your time and do it right the first time, it won't take you as long to get it done."

Submitted by Kelli T.

"I wait for the Lord, my soul does wait, And in His word do I hope." Psalms 130:5 NASB1995

"Blessed is a man who perseveres under trial; for once he has been approved, he will receive the crown of life which the Lord has promised to those who love Him." James 1:12 NASB 1995

"For I consider that the sufferings of this present time are not worthy to be compared with the glory that is to be revealed to us." Romans 8:18 NASB1995

NOTES:

_____

_____

_____

_____

_____

_____

_____

_____

_____

_____

_____

_____

_____

_____

_____

CHAPTER EIGHT

STRENGTH

For as long as I can remember, my uncle Fred has always been a hard-working man. He grew up in Rineyville, KY and worked and retired as a door-to-door mail carrier for the United States Postal Service. My favorite thing about my uncle Fred is he had a laugh that would fill the room, robust, loud, and long. He had arms that would hug the air right out of you. No matter how old we were, he always had hugs for us. I spent many nights at their house, and he always let me help them with chores and farm work. He taught me how to ride a horse bareback. I loved spending summers with them! I truly believed growing up, his remedy for all ailments was salve; cut your finger half off topping tobacco; use salve; have a splinter; use salve; got a wart-use salve. Our families used to grow tobacco together. I remember several times he would drive the truck to the ends of the rows and turn on the headlights so my dad could drive the tractor so we could finish setting, even if it was midnight. Fred was always one to joke around and I loved the brotherly relationship he had with my father. For several years, his family and mine would go rough camping at Land Between the Lakes. Without fail, we would all pile in the back of the trucks and make the trek there. Backroads with no signs and never a map, Fred could find the spot we always camped at like he had lived there his whole life. He never got lost, until Dementia took over his life. I love that man and always will even when he doesn't remember my name.

Submitted by Tracy G.

"I have seen that nothing is better than that man should be happy in his activities, for that is his lot. For who will bring him to see what will occur after him?" Ecclesiastes 3:22 NASB1995

"A friend loves at all times, And a brother is born for adversity." Proverbs 17:17 NASB1995

"Let the favor of the Lord our God be upon us; And confirm for us the work of our hands; Yes, confirm the work of our hands." Psalms 90:17 NASB1995

NOTES:

_____

_____

_____

_____

_____

_____

_____

_____

_____

_____

When I think of my favorite memories of Donnie, I remember one afternoon in December 2007. I stopped by the shop one afternoon to see Roy. Donnie walked out of his office, put his hands on his hips and asked, "What are you doing here"? I said, "I'm here to see you." He looked kind of sideways at me and asked, "What for?" I said, "Because you like me!" He stood there thinking for a minute and finally said, "Well okay, I guess I do since you told me I have to like you!" From that day on for several years this was a running joke between him and I. He got a kick out of saying, "I like you because you told me I had to like you!"

Submitted by Missy B.

"The name of the Lord is a strong tower; The righteous runs into it and is safe." Proverbs 18:10 NASB1995

"Finally, be strong in the Lord and in the strength of His might." Ephesians 6:10 NASB1995

"He who is slow to anger is better than the mighty, And he who rules his spirit, than he who captures a city." Proverbs 16:32 NASB1995

NOTES:

Memories

I've sat here attempting this many times with little to no success of where to start writing my most fond memories of my grandfather, better known to me as Dee Dee. How does one place a lifetime of cherished memories in a few hundred words? I'd say it's nearly impossible to encapsulate what it was like to experience life growing up with my Dee Dee.

Some of my favorite memories include the time spent around a dinner table every Sunday evening, and his quick witty remarks in a conversation. I loved getting dropped off at his work after school and him teaching me how to play solitaire on his computer. I also enjoyed walking up to the barns at my grandparent's house and listening to him talk about cars; the make, model and details that make it worth having. Nothing was better than sitting and watching him tinker on his car or whatever needed fixing. The best was walking into my grandparent's house and being greeted by "hey there legs," because I was a skinny long-legged child. These are merely glimmers in time.

Though dementia has stolen his memories of us and who we are, he's still quick with a joke. He still calls me "legs" or some similar nickname, and he can still talk for hours about cars. Pieces of who he used to be remain. The sentences may not come out right, it may take longer to tell a joke, but the man I knew before is still there. The memories mean more to me now that he can no longer recall all of them. I will carry the gift of time spent with my grandfather forever.

Submitted by Emilee J.

"Seek the Lord and His strength; Seek His face continually." 1 Chronicles 16:11 NASB1995

"God is our refuge and strength, A very present help in trouble." Psalms 46:1 NASB1995

"He gives strength to the weary, And to him who lacks might He increases power." Isaiah 40:29 NASB1995

NOTES:

_____

_____

_____

_____

_____

_____

_____

_____

_____

_____

_____

_____

_____

The Ultimate Sacrifice

Mom did not have the best luck with love and family. She was abused at a very young age by a family member. She then went straight into a difficult marriage, trying to raise two young children with little help from an alcoholic husband. More times than not, Mom would go without her basic needs so we could have the things we needed, while not knowing how she would make rent and feed the kids.

Later, Mom found herself in another marriage filled with infidelity and mental abuse, also bringing another mouth to feed into an already strained situation. Mom was a strong and determined woman whose only goal was to see that her children had a roof over their heads and food on the table. Mom knew sacrifice all too well, sometimes working two jobs to make ends meet. One of her jobs involved working with elderly dementia patients at a nursing home.

By the time she settled into her third and final marriage my brother and I were out on our own, but her youngest daughter thought of him as her dad. Life was looking up for her. She loved Disney World and was able to go several times. Family was important and Mom loved the holidays and cooking for everyone. We would go for drives in the country, and she would show us where she used to live and tell so many stories. Grand kids were her life and spending time with them was priceless to her. She also loved her animals and enjoyed grooming and taking care of them.

In January 2014 she was diagnosed with Alzheimer's. She knew firsthand what that diagnosis meant. We gathered the immediate family up and told them the news. After this, we could never make plans with her because she would make herself physically ill from worrying. All our friends would come to our house to hang out with us so we wouldn't have to leave Mom.

On September 30, 2014, at age sixty-nine, my mom took her own life. She left us a note explaining why she did it. She sacrificed herself for her family because she said she wanted to give us our life back. She also said she made her peace with God. She is finally at peace. She made the "Ultimate Sacrifice". I just miss you, Mom.

Submitted by Tilina G.

"After you have suffered for a little while, the God of all grace, who called you to His eternal glory in Christ, will Himself perfect, confirm, strengthen and establish you." 1 Peter 5:10 NASB 1995

"Come to Me, all who are weary and heavy-laden, and I will give you rest. Take My yoke upon you and learn from Me, for I am gentle and humble in heart, and you will find rest for your souls." Matthew 11:28-29 NASB1995

"The Lord is near to the brokenhearted And saves those who are crushed in spirit." Psalms 34:18 NASB1995

NOTES:

CHAPTER NINE

COURAGE

Alisha J. story of her Mamaw

"Hello. I had just laid my phone down." I heard the excitement in her voice every time I would call. "Mamaw, I have kidney stones and I need to go to the hospital. Can you please come to my house and take care of Curtis?"

Mamaw didn't drive in the snow. She never had. And it was snowing like crazy. "Oh, no! Let me start the car, I'll be there as soon as I can." You could hear the panic in her voice. Curtis was her world. He was the first and only great grandchild. They had a special bond. She would keep him while I worked and would do anything for him.

Mamaw lived about ten minutes away, when driving under the speed limit and with all the traffic. But this day, she made it to my house in twelve minutes, even with the snow-covered roads. She swung her door open as I walked outside.

"The roads are slick, but Curtis needs me!" She rushed to get out of the car and in the front door. As she opened it, Curtis came running with a big hug for her. This is just a small thing that this disease has taken from me and my family.

Submitted by Alisha J.

"Be strong and let your heart take courage, All you who hope in the Lord." Psalms 31:24 NASB1995

"'Do not fear, for I am with you; Do not anxiously look about you, for I am your God. I will strengthen you, surely I will help you, Surely I will uphold you with My righteous right hand." Isaiah 41:10 NASB

"Have I not commanded you? Be strong and courageous! Do not tremble or be dismayed, for the Lord your God is with you wherever you go." Joshua 1:9 NASB1995

NOTES:

_____

_____

_____

_____

_____

_____

_____

_____

_____

_____

_____

_____

_____

_____

My Dad, Then and Now

Dad is now two different men. Growing up he worked a lot, starting his own business, he was a very driven man. He could do anything and if something was broken, he would figure out how to fix it whether it be a tractor, car roof, changing out a water heater, work on the furnace, or changing out faucets. This is just some of the things he has done for me throughout my life.

Dad also had plain old common sense, which a lot of people lack these days. He also taught my son so much about life. He taught him a great work ethic, but they also spent a lot of time playing golf. Apparently, Dad created a monster in that regard, because my son loves golf a lot, but back in the day, my dad did too. I remember my mom and dad started to play golf for the exercise. They walked the course, no cart riding.

My dad was not one to show emotions or say "I love you" but we knew he did by the way he took care of us and provided a good life for us. Later, as his business did well, he would buy fun things for us to do as a family. A boat, camper to go camping, and snowmobiles. That's how he showed his love for us.

Now days, my dad tells me he loves me more than ever in my life. He shows more emotions to my mom, us kids and of course, the grandkids and great-grand kids.

To me, there are pros and cons to this disease. When I started noticing him being forgetful or having that far off look, we knew something was changing. I prayed that if he was to get this terrible disease, that at least he would be a calmer person and not violent. At this stage of the game, God has granted me this wish. He is now like a child, confused, but to me, he's happy and that is all I can ask for.

What gives him the most joy is when the great-grandkids or my grand-dog, come over to visit, he is just happy and laughing. You know, at this point, that is all I pray for!

I won't say that there haven't been many challenges, but my Moto is "One day at a time" and "This too shall pass." I know his demeanor can change but for today, it's not too bad. I can see the dementia is progressing. This time last year we would have gone for car rides, which he enjoyed, now he is scared cars are gonna hit us.

Sometimes I look at him and I remember the man he was, but that person is gone. It is sad. I still love him, regardless, especially since he is kinder. I'm not sure what's down the road but will take it "One Day at a Time".

Love You Dad, Andrea

Submitted by Andrea B.

"Be strong and courageous, do not be afraid or tremble at them, for the Lord your God is the one who goes with you. He will not fail you or forsake you." Deuteronomy 31:6 NASB1995

"Though a host encamp against me, My heart will not fear; Though war arise against me, In spite of this I shall be confident." Psalms 27:3 NASB1995

"Fight the good fight of faith; take hold of the eternal life to which you were called, and you made the good confession in the presence of many witnesses." 1 Timothy 6:12 NASB1995

NOTES:

_____

_____

_____

_____

_____

_____

_____

_____

_____

_____

_____

_____

_____

_____

_____

_____

_____

_____

_____

_____

_____

The loss and void of a parent never goes away.

I may have lost my daddy to Alzheimer's twenty-eight years ago, but I have so many fond, fun, and sincere memories. I believe memories are what keeps traditions alive and a family line strong.

My dad, Joe, worked hard his whole life. He lived by the motto "you work hard to be able to have the best things in life." And he always had the best of the best. One of my favorite memories is of his CB radio set up. He loved to talk nightly to his friends and attend monthly weekend radio jamborees. I was between the ages of ten and twelve and I'd love to listen to him, and his friend swap stories, trade postcards and listen to him come across the radio waves as KRJ2495/Skunk Holler. CB radio was texting before cellular phones were even a thing!

We had a cabin at Nolin Lake. We worked hard with chores and mowing to then enjoy our pontoon, trotline fishing and enjoying our "best of the best" boating dock.

My daddy couldn't tell a joke to save his life. This is only because he got so tickled himself before he even got to the punchline. I can still clearly hear his laugh to this day.

He worked hard at Knox Motor Ford in Fort Knox. I can remember going to work with him when I was between the ages of nine and ten years old. My kids would say I get my work ethic from him.

He had a superstition of not walking out the door he didn't come in. He had a substantial collection of belt buckles; he didn't wear a button up if it didn't have pearl snaps and he always kept a comb close by for his comb-over. He always chewed just a half a stick of juicy fruit chewing gum.

Alzheimer's took him from us just a short seven and a half years after he was diagnosed. I think he also died of a broken heart just ten weeks after his beloved wife of 60 years, Ruby, passed away.

Cherish your parents, ask for stories, and always tell them you love them.

Submitted by Rick N. & Emily J.

"Therefore, being always of good courage, and knowing that while we are at home in the body we are absent from the Lord- for we walk by faith, not by sight-" 2 Corinthians 5:6-7 NASB1995

"Even though I walk through the valley of the shadow of death, I fear no evil, for You are with me; Your rod and Your staff, they comfort me." Psalms 23:4 NASB1995

"When I am afraid, I will put my trust in You. In God, whose word I praise, In God I have put my trust; I shall not be afraid. What can mere man do to me?" Psalms 56:3-4 NASB1995

NOTES:

CHAPTER TEN

GRATITUDE

I am so thankful for my sweet, precious, smiling, praying, loving momma. She doesn't know many of us anymore, but she recognizes our faces sometimes. She no longer can talk on the phone or carry on a conversation that makes sense. She barely can hear but mostly not. Sometimes I see her staring at something or someone and I can only imagine what she's trying to remember. Momma has always prayed she would see all her kids and grandchildren saved. She often sits and sleeps but sometimes you will walk into the room to find her praying or trying to remember a song. She will have her hands raised to Heaven praising her Lord and Savior. I would always go to mom to pray for me for whatever I needed. She always went to God first! It hasn't been long since she laid hands on me and prayed. That's one thing she instilled in me, go to God first. When she's having a good day, I can say, "I love you, Momma" and she says, "I love you too". Then I say, "I love you more", and she says, "Oh no you don't", and smiles so big. She says, "I always wanted a little girl and God finally gave me you". I'm named after my momma, Dixie Louise. I'm Glenda Louise. I know she recognizes me when I see her smile and the twinkle in her eyes, and I'm home. I know soon she will get what she's been longing for all her life, Heaven. She'll make it home. I love you momma...I am so blessed to call her mom. Thank you, Lord, for my precious Mom.

Five children, eight grandchildren, eighteen great-grandchildren. Homemaker, church song leader, Sunday school teacher, mentor to many, played and sang at nursing homes over twenty years. Truly loved her Jesus. A very special lady.

Submitted by Glenda D.

"I have no greater joy than this, to hear of my children walking in the truth." 3 John 1:4 NASB1995

"Therefore be imitators of God, as beloved children; and walk in love, just as Christ also loved you and gave Himself up for us, an offering and a sacrifice to God as a fragrant aroma." Ephesians 5:1-2 NASB1995

"Rejoice always; pray without ceasing; in everything give thanks; for this is God's will for you in Christ Jesus." 1 Thessalonians 5:16-18 NASB1995

NOTES:

_____

_____

_____

_____

_____

_____

_____

_____

_____

_____

Dad wasn't the hunter, but he was always there for the hunt. He would drive us to our spot and pick us up when we were done.

Dad changed the hunt.

Breakfast would be waiting in the morning with supper in the evening.

Dad changed the hunt.

He would be as excited as we were for a harvested deer, although he couldn't linger long with the allergies that would flare but was always right there waiting to help bring it in and hang it in the air.

Dad changed the hunt.

Times have changed with dad not here and the joy of the hunt has just disappeared.

Dad changed the hunt.

The anticipation and excitement of the hunt went far beyond the hunt itself. It was the gathering of family, sharing of stories, and building of relationships.

Dad changed the hunt.

Memories remain in the vastness of my mind, but the desire of the hunt has passed away with him because Dad changed the hunt.

I still love to hunt but I can't bring myself to go. It's in this loss I've discovered that it wasn't so much the hunting that I anticipated but it was the hunt, time with family and my dad because, Dad changed the hunt.

Submitted by Deric P.

"Hope deferred makes the heart sick, But desire fulfilled is a tree

of life." Proverbs 13:12 NASB1995

"As the deer pants for the water brooks, So my soul pants for You, O God." Psalms 42:1 NASB1995

"You have taken account of my wanderings; Put my tears in Your bottle. Are they not in Your book?" Psalms 56:8 NASB1995

NOTES:

_____

_____

_____

_____

_____

_____

_____

_____

_____

_____

_____

_____

_____

_____

When I think of my DeeDee.....

I have always looked at my DeeDee with inspiration and admiration. Not only did he start a business from the ground up, but he has also maintained a successful business for almost sixty years. He is an 82-year-old man, who doesn't need to, but wants to, get up every day and still go to work. He has built something from nothing, and I admire him so much for that. He has always been hilarious, a prankster, a jokester, someone who loves to laugh and someone who can always make you laugh. I remember being little, and he would hide our Easter eggs in the sticker bushes around the yard. When we would yawn, he would stick his big old sausage link finger in our throats, and he would laugh so hard when it made us gag. He would give us "Indian burn" on our wrist and "milk your mouse" on our pinkies. He has always shown us tough love.

He's always made jokes and called us questionable nicknames, that only he could get away with. But the truth is, we've loved it because we've always known, that his way of showing love and affection, and always has been in a very rare and resilient way. I have always looked at my DeeDee as being one of the strongest and toughest men that I know. Although, he has a side to him that is a big teddy bear. This came out even more when he had great grandkids. I've absolutely loved watching his face light up, just by being around the little ones. No matter what's going on, they can always make him laugh. You can just tell how proud he is to be a great grandpa, and I am so excited and grateful to be able to see him have these same interactions with my little one this year. My DeeDee is a rare breed, they just don't make them like that anymore. A strong, ambitious man, who can turn from a serious businessman one minute, to a sweet old grandpa the next. I can honestly say that I have always felt special because I know that nobody has a grandpa like we do. And now comes the hard part. I've been aware of the disease responsible for the deterioration of the mind, known as Alzheimer's. But I've never had someone I love who's personally been affected by it. To say it is heartbreaking to watch, is an understatement. To see a man who has always been so strong and full of life, get scattered and confused in the middle of a conversation or situation is an extremely hard thing to deal with, much less to accept. I know how much my grandma, my mom, my aunt, and my uncle do for him daily, but the truth is I'm not on the frontline to experience the pain and heartache like they do every day. Unfortunately, there is no known cure, and it is a disease that will continue to progress. Even having to write those words, absolutely terrifies me because we are all helpless to stop it from continuing to take away from a man, who I've always known could face anything or anyone. I've read about it, and I've done my research, to not only educate myself about this disease but to also learn the best ways to handle interactions with him. Sadly, playing along and not drawing attention to the fact that he is confused, has been the best advice I have found. Because at times, they might not know that they have something affecting their memory and communication skills, but at other times they are very aware, and that is the hardest part to see. However, I can honestly say, that this unfortunate circumstance has not changed the way I look at my sweet DeeDee, not even for a second. If anything, it's taught me that life is going to throw you curveballs, but you can't let the impact of the hit alter your strength, your faith, or your perseverance. It has shown me, that life is short and unpredictable but, in every situation, we can choose to find the blessings and the gratitude within it. For example, I take more pictures and videos, so that I will always have those memories with him to cherish. I soak up every smile, every laugh, every hug, every joke, because I know that they are priceless treasures. I pray for him and my family, to keep our faith in God that he will help guide us on this journey. And at the end of day, I will always be so incredibly grateful to God for giving me such a smart, unique, hilarious, amazing man that I've been lucky enough to call my DeeDee.

Submitted by Samantha R.

"Whatever you do in word or deed, do all in the name of the Lord Jesus, giving thanks through Him to God the Father." Colossians 3:17 NASB1995

"O give thanks to the Lord, for He is good; For His lovingkindness is everlasting." 1 Chronicles 16:34 NASB1995

"I will give thanks to You, for I am fearfully and wonderfully made; Wonderful are Your works, And my soul knows it very well." Psalms 139:14 NASB1995

NOTES:

CHAPTER ELEVEN

JOY

August 4, 1926 - March 14, 2006

This picture is my father on his wedding day to Geneva, April 3, 1953. He was a man who went to work everyday and made sure his family was taken care of.

After settling into his last home in Louisville, he got into the sport of stock car racing. Along with brothers and friends. To this day I am an avid fan of Nascar, thanks to him.

After his parents retired to Nelson County, he made his weekend time to be there for gardening, shade-tree mechanics, and general home repairs. It was also a time when his extended family would gather. Nothing meant more to him than his family. His favorite times were vacations in the country when brothers would come home from out of state. Then there were family reunions. I loved when he would introduce me to all his aunts, uncles, cousins, and some old friends.

In 2001 dad was diagnosed with dementia. I had seen it coming with his off-the-wall talk and words I had never heard him use. He knew something was wrong. He told me, "You know, sometimes I forget things and sometimes I remember." I tried to play it off as we all do that. His knowing everyday things went fast. But he was able to remember life of years ago. Fortunately, he never got the mean or nasty personality which can sometimes take over some.

The one thing I can still hear today is daddy's laugh. He laughed at anything, and we laughed at him. Even through the heartbreaking disease, he laughed.

Submitted by Vickie P.

"A joyful heart makes a cheerful face, But when the heart is sad, the spirit is broken." Proverbs 15:13 NASB1995

"Bright eyes gladden the heart; Good news puts fat on the bones." Proverbs 15:30 NASB1995

"A joyful heart is good medicine, But a broken spirit dries up the bones." Proverbs 17:22 NASB1995

NOTES:

_____

_____

_____

_____

_____

_____

_____

_____

_____

_____

_____

_____

_____

Mom was a spunky, fun-loving lady. She had such a sweet smile and almost bashful demeanor. She loved taking long shopping trips that involved eating out. One Saturday on our way home from a fun afternoon, I was driving her car. I pushed the CD player button, and it was such a shock hearing Lady Gaga's "Poker Face". Mom noticed my shock and sheepishly smiled. I said, "Lady Gaga"? She asked what was wrong with that? I told her nothing, but I was shocked because I expected George Jones or someone. She said that I should see her when she gets to dancing. She was a beautiful woman, full of life and a sparkling personality.

Submitted by Angie G.

"A time to weep and a time to laugh; A time to mourn and a time to dance." Ecclesiastes 3:4 NASB1995

"Rejoice in the Lord always; again I will say, rejoice!" Philippians 4:4 NASB1995

"This is the day which the Lord has made; Let us rejoice and be glad in it." Psalms 118:24 NASB1995

NOTES:

I really struggled to come up with something and put it into words but here is my best attempt.

Moving away after college, many things changed. One that stayed constant was Christmas Eve at Grandma's house when she would cook a big meal for our family. Over time the tradition has changed slightly. Grandma hasn't cooked a big meal in a long time, opting now to order "the best pizza... period." But getting together as a family has not changed. Even now that she is in assisted living, we still can get together... and grandma got to make an appearance this year.

Submitted by Courtney H.

"But the fruit of the Spirit is love, joy, peace, patience, kindness, goodness, faithfulness, gentleness, self-control; against such things there is no law." Galatians 5:22-23 NASB1995

"Now may the God of hope fill you with all joy and peace in believing, so that you will abound in hope by the power of the Holy Spirit." Romans 15:13 NASB1995

"Then he said to them, "Go, eat of the fat, drink of the sweet, and send portions to him who has nothing prepared; for this day is holy to our Lord. Do not be grieved, for the joy of the Lord is your strength."" Nehemiah 8:10 NASB1995

NOTES:

CHAPTER TWELVE

PEACE

Virginia, mother to Sherry, Tim, Carlena, and Pam, was a wonderful lady with a smile that would light up the room. As young children, all four of us siblings did not live in the same house together but we all clearly have the same memories of our mother. When we were young children, we remember she sang to us. She sang when we were happy, sad, or scared. She sang a lot of songs but the song we remember most of all was "You are My Sunshine." This song brought her happiness and brought us happiness. We also know that she sang it to her grandchildren.

When her disease became more progressed, the tables simply turned, and we sang to her. When she was agitated and could not explain her thoughts, we sang. When she was happy and seemed like she remembered us, we sang. When she sat in silence and showed no emotion, we sang. We sang "You are My Sunshine" and it appeared to calm her. We sang it daily when we were at the nursing home with her.

She was and remains the sunshine to her entire family. She just shines from Heaven now.

Submitted by Carlena S., Tim A., Pam B., and Sherry C.

"The Lord is my strength and my shield; My heart trusts in Him, and I am helped; Therefore my heart exults, And with my song I shall thank Him." Psalms 28:7 NASB1995

"Sing for joy in the Lord, O you righteous ones; Praise is becoming to the upright." Psalms 33:1 NASB1995

"O come, let us sing for joy to the Lord, Let us shout joyfully to the rock of our salvation. Let us come before His presence with thanksgiving, Let us shout joyfully to Him with psalms." Psalms 95:1-2 NASB1995

NOTES:

_____

_____

_____

_____

_____

_____

_____

_____

_____

_____

_____

_____

_____

_____

_____

Marvin was a terrific guy. He loved his family. He loved being active and was a pitcher on my kids' ball team when they were young. He had a good sense of humor and loved to drive fast. When Pop first began not being Pop, one Saturday morning he disappeared. We looked everywhere and he was finally found in Boston, nearly seven miles from home. He had walked the railroad tracks. We were worried to death, but he thought it was funny. The next time he disappeared he was lost in the woods. After hours of looking for him, he was finally found behind a neighbor's house. He looked like he had been in a fight with a bear. He was taken to the hospital where he was later diagnosed with dementia.

Submitted by Annette S.

"Do not let your heart be troubled; believe in God, believe also in Me. In My Father's house are many dwelling places; if it were not so, I would have told you; for I go to prepare a place for you. If I go and prepare a place for you, I will come again and receive you to Myself, that where I am, there you may be also." John 14:1-3 NASB1995

"Be anxious for nothing, but in everything by prayer and supplication with thanksgiving let your requests be made known to God. And the peace of God, which surpasses all comprehension, will guard your hearts and your minds in Christ Jesus." Philippians 4:6-7 NASB

"The Lord is my shepherd, I shall not want. He makes me lie down in green pastures; He leads me beside quiet waters. He restores my soul; He guides me in the paths of righteousness For His name's sake." Psalms 23:1-3 NASB1995

NOTES:

_____

_____

_____

_____

_____

_____

_____

_____

_____

_____

_____

_____

_____

_____

_____

_____

_____

_____

_____

_____

Mamaw used to keep me when my Momma was at work. My mom worked different shifts at a nursing home. I always slept in the same bed Mamaw did. She used to play games with me and when it was warm, she would play outside in the mud with me, with my trucks and cars. Mamaw had an entertainment center that had cabinets at the bottom where I would hide when I stayed with her.

Submitted by Curtis M.

"Peace I leave with you; My peace I give to you; not as the world gives do I give to you. Do not let your heart be troubled, nor let it be fearful." John 14:27 NASB1995

"The Lord bless you, and keep you; The Lord make His face shine on you, And be gracious to you; The Lord lift up His countenance on you, And give you peace." Numbers 6:24-2 NASB1995

"You are my hiding place; You preserve me from trouble; You surround me with songs of deliverance." Psalms 32:7 NASB1995

NOTES:

Alzheimer's has affected my family for many years. I lost my great grandfather to the disease in 1987. But it wasn't until 2016 when I lost my Great Aunt, Wilma Jean, to Alzheimer's that I saw just how devastating it's affects can be on a human being.

Although she was my Great Aunt, Wilma and I were like best friends. There were many years between us in age, but it didn't matter. She told me I was an old soul. We did many things together when she would come in to visit my family and me. When I would see her after some time had passed, she would always ask me, "Are you happy?" I always obliged and told her I was. During the late evening hours near sundown, we would go for walks, and we would talk about life. I remember once stopping in the middle of a huge field of wildflowers and we tried to count all the fireflies flying around us. It felt so magical. We truly were the best of friends.

When I married and moved away, I didn't see my Wilma very often but when I did, it was like old times. In the summer of 2001 things began to change. Wilma and my mother came to visit my wife and I at our apartment to see our newborn baby girl. I was so happy to see her, but something just didn't seem right. She wasn't herself and she was somewhat distant. Later Mom told me Wilma had been diagnosed with early onset dementia. Mom said that Wilma had the best doctors, and her medication would most likely slow the progression of her disease. I remember calling her to see how she was doing, and she always seemed to be doing well.

In 2015, I saw my aunt for the very last time. We were attending a family reunion. I was so excited to see her, but it really was a very somber occasion. When my aunt arrived, she literally knew no one. She was scared and kept saying she wanted to go home. My heart sank. It had been a long while since I had seen her, and I just couldn't grasp how much her disease had worsened to the point she knew absolutely no one. That was the last time I saw my aunt. On the drive home, I sobbed like a baby. How could someone so smart and so sophisticated, who had such a passion for life, get to a point where they knew no one. I was devastated. That was the day I realized how horrific Alzheimer's was.

In January 2016, My Great Aunt, Wilma Jean, passed away after having fought a long, hard battle against Alzheimer's. Alzheimer's slowly took everything away from her. The Wilma I knew many years prior to Alzheimer's was gone. She's certainly not forgotten, and I'll always love her. If she could ask me today if I was happy, I'd tell her when a cure is found for Alzheimer's then I will be genuinely happy for those who are going through this terrible disease.

Submitted by Brent C.

"These things I have spoken to you, so that in Me you may have peace. In the world you have tribulation, but take courage; I have overcome the world." John 16:33 NASB1995

"Now may the Lord of peace Himself continually grant you peace in every circumstance. The Lord be with you all!" 2 Thessalonians 3:16 NASB1995

"The Lord will give strength to His people; The Lord will bless His people with peace." Psalms 29:11 NASB1995

NOTES:

_____

_____
_____
_____
_____
_____
_____
_____
_____
_____
_____
_____
_____
_____
_____
_____
_____
_____
_____
_____
_____

DE DE COX

Born and raised on the farm in Rooster Run, Kentucky, de de was raised on the core values of the 3Cs (kindness, caring, and compassion). Throughout her young adulthood, de de volunteered in the community with her family, and specifically, her grandmother, Bea. Growing up in the country, romance novels were her escape to another world. de de knew that one day, her dream of writing would come true. Fast forward to 2018, when de de picked the book back up that she had begun in her early 30s. As in life, circumstances and direction change the course, BUT never the ending goal. Learning the industry and working with her publisher, Beyond Global Publishing, God opened many doors and many connections, and de de has never looked back.

de de became a published Kentucky romance author in 2018. She is the #1 best-selling Kentucky romance author of the Two Degrees Series, which features her son, Bo, as the male model. Little did de de know that her child would become the next FabiBo.

de de is working on her new series – RESCUE ME (animals and love), which debuted in 2021. The story of rescue, the story of love, the story of FURever.

de de has served as a board member of The Dream Factory of Louisville, KY, Opal's Dream Foundation, Spalding University –

Athletic Board, as well as volunteered with other charitable entities. de de received the coveted 2018 Spirit of Louisville Foundation - WLKY Bell Award for her volunteerism within her community and now serves on the board as trustee.

de de is active within the pageant industry. She is the co-preliminary director of the Miss My Old Kentucky Home (a prelim to the state /national of the Miss America system). In addition, she is the co-director of the Miss Hillview, Miss Buttermilk, and Miss Bullitt Blast Festival prelims (Kentucky State Festival).

FAMILY (family always mean I love you) and this is true in de de's life. So many kind-hearted folks have traveled the journey. She has been married for over Thirty-five years to her best friend, Scott, from high school. She has two sons and two rescued fur babies.

De De encourages others to live by HIS word – Acts 20:35.

DEAN PARRISH

Dean grew up in the heart of Central Kentucky in rural Nelson County. Being raised in a Christian home and growing up poor, he learned early in life the value of faith, family, integrity, and hard work. With the heart of a servant and a passion for people, Dean has spent over thirty years working as a professional sales consultant. He has been married to his beautiful wife, Beverly, for over 30 years. He is a devoted father of seven, and grandfather to a growing number of grandchildren. In addition to working a full-time job, Dean has worked in his church as a deacon, teacher, and worship leader. He has also worked in his community as an assistant coach for middle school football and little league baseball. He loves a challenge and once ran a half-marathon because his wife told him she didn't think he could do it. His deepest devotion and highest priorities are given to God, his wife and growing family. Successfully raising his six daughters and one son, has been the greatest and most rewarding challenge in his life.

Dean enjoys writing and has written and published three other books. His first book, "In Search of Truth" is a faith-based book and he also has published two children's books in the "Life in Shannondale" series, "Goatie the B-a-a-a-d Goat" and "Goatie Throws a Party". He is very excited to be a part of his most recent collaboration on this book to honor the memory of his father who he lost to Alzheimer's.

DONETTA BENNETT HARNED

Donetta was born, raised and never left the quiet, small town called Bardstown, Kentucky, that she calls home. She grew up in an area that was peaceful, slow, and laid back.

She was blessed with two wonderful parents and a supportive sister and brother. She is the wife of a wonderful and supportive husband, mother of four beautiful, grown daughters, great son-in-laws, and Nana to four awesome grandsons. She is also aunt to some very special nieces and nephews. Family has always been very important to her.

She has been a licensed cosmologist for almost 40 years, worked in the dental field for over 25 years, and is now working at the family-owned, lawn-mowing equipment business to finish up her working career.

Some call her a workaholic, but she really enjoys staying busy, socially active, and meeting people. Donetta gives thanks to God for her life full of blessings and she finds inspiration through scripture like the one she shares below.

"I can do all things through Christ who strengthens me." Philippians 4:13

www.ingramcontent.com/pod-product-compliance
Lightning Source LLC
LaVergne TN
LVHW011838060526
838200LV00053B/4081